Photo Ark
ABC

An **Animal Alphabet** in **Poetry** and **Pictures**

Photographs by
Joel Sartore
Photo Ark Creator

Poems by
Debbie Levy

NATIONAL GEOGRAPHIC
Washington, D.C.

Hi, Armadillo!
Greetings, Grizzly Bear!
n a poem you are neighbors.
n the wild, you're not a pair.

Good day, graceful Crane,
And Duckling of webbed feet,
Oh, Elephant-enormous!
Yo, leap-Froggy petite!

Hey, Grouper (who would rather swim
Alone than in a group),
Hyena, hanging with your clan,
Calling *WHOOP! WHOOP! WHOOP!*

guana, Jelly, Katydid,
n mountain, sea, and tree,
Mighty Lion claims the plains—
Who dares to disagree?

Howdy, Monkey, in the vines,
And you, Newt, by the pond,
Octopus from ocean shallows
To the depths beyond,

Panda, Quoll, so different
Yet alike—you're both so cute!
Rhino, Spider, what a team:
Twelve legs and such a snoot!

Buenos días, Tapir,
Urial, **hello!**
Vulture, Walrus, have you met?
(The answer's likely "no.")

Xenarthrans, you're a trio,
Three critters with one name,
There's room for you, and Yabby, too,
And join us, Zebra, please—who knew
This Photo Ark could be so jammed
With fascinating creatures crammed
But just a tiny fraction of
The life that swims, and flies above,
And walks and crawls and runs and . . .
WOW!
Let's turn the page—

The Ark sails NOW.

A

is for Armadillo

Armadillo

Is a pillow

Or . . . a stone? A scone?

So still—OH!

Not so still—

What's that inside?

A snout, four legs, a tail—

Don't hide!

4

Now uncurling,
Now uncurled,
Standing to **explore**
The world.

The only mammal
With a **shell**
Can barely see,
But sure can smell.

A sniff will tell
If danger's near
And if it's time
To **disappear** ...

To once again Become a **pillow,**
Stony, scone-y
Armadillo.

B is for Bear and Butterfly

Summer and fall, Grizzly Bear
Feasts and feasts and feasts
On caribou, moose, elk, and deer,
Beasts and beasts and BEASTS,

On fruits and fish, roots and berries,
Heaps and heaps and heaps,
Then winter comes, and Grizzly Bear
Sleeps and sleeps and Sleeps...

~

When Grizzly Bear awakens from
Sleeping, sleeping, sleeping
Somewhere there's a Caterpillar
Creeping, creeping, creeping.

Caterpillar eats and eats
Leaves and leaves and leaves.
When it's full it sews a sack—

Weaves and weaves and weaves.

Wait a while and from the sack,
Soaring, soaring, soaring,
The bug becomes a Butterfly!

Explore, explore, exploring.

C is for Crane

This **crown** is fit for a king, a queen

Abuela, bubbe
Auntie, uncle
Crane.

A fresh haircut
Without hair,
A cap without a brim,
Braids without twists,
Electricity
Without current, but

Stunning.

Oh, you Crane:

Hats off
To you.

Hey, little Duckling,
What did you do?

What's that **drop**

I see behind **you?**

D
is for
Duck

Aw, little Mallard,
That's part of life, too—
Not just a **Duck thing,**
It's what we all do!

That trunk!

E is for Elephant

A hose,
A nose,
Reaching food that **grows**
From treetops down to toes,

That **trunk!**

Moves dirt,
And **squirts,**
Snuffs water up to sip,
Holds objects in its grip,

That **trunk!**

A shower
With power,
A tool
SO COOL!

That **trunk!**

F is for Frog

A worm, a bug, a fly, a slug—
A Frog will eat them all.
Slurp! snaps the tongue.
Glug! gulps the Frog.

A Frog will eat them all—
Spiders, eggs, tiny fish.
Glug! gulps the Frog.
Down!
go
the

Spiders, eggs, tiny fish.
All swallowed whole.
Down!
go
the
Squirmy, crawly, squiggly dinners

All swallowed whole.
Anything alive, anything that fits—
Squirmy, crawly, squiggly dinners,
A Frog will **eat them all.**

Change is the name
of Grouper's
GAME:

G
is for
Grouper

Tiny to **tubby,**
Blotchy to spotty,
White to gray,

And—switcheroo!—

Female to **male,**
All in a single fish.
All in a single **life.**

H is for Hyena

After the **big hunt**
Who will pitch in to **clean up?**

Others eat and run
But Hyena shows up late
And puts **away leftovers.**

15

Up in the **trees**
A blue-green **gem,**
Treasure among **leaves,**
A **jewel** on a branch.

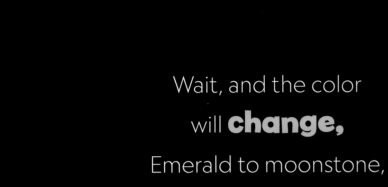

Wait, and the color
will **change,**
Emerald to moonstone,
Bright to shadow, sun to shade
And **back again.**

I
is for
Iguana

Neither emerald nor **moonstone,**
Not mineral, but **fauna,**

This gem has a **backbone**
This gem is **IGUANA.**

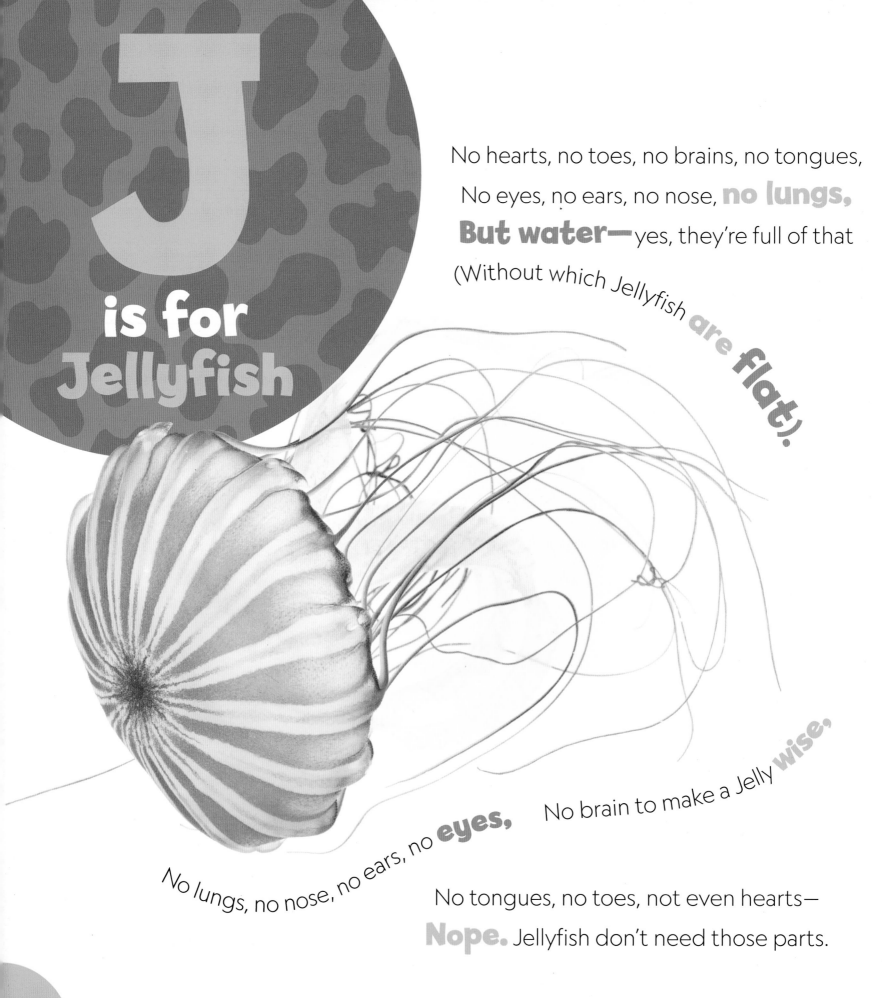

J is for Jellyfish

No hearts, no toes, no brains, no tongues,
No eyes, no ears, no nose, **no lungs,**
But water—yes, they're full of that
(Without which Jellyfish **are flat).**

No lungs, no nose, no ears, no **eyes,**
No brain to make a Jelly **wise,**

No tongues, no toes, not even hearts—
Nope. Jellyfish don't need those parts.

Katy do, Katy don't

Katy does, Katy won't

Katy can't, Katy shan't

Katy can, Katy shall

Join the **Katydid chorale,**

K

is for

Katydid

Singing

Katydid-*she*-**didn't**-

She-**did**-*she*-**didn't**-

She-**did**-*she*-**didn't**-*she*-**did**-*she*-**didn't**-

All night long.

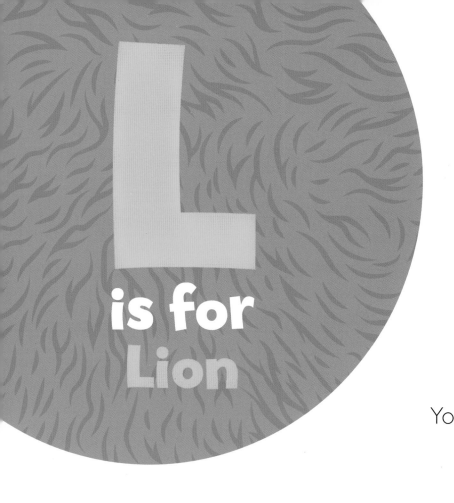

L is for Lion

Lion, Lion, lyin' there
Lyin' like you have no care,
Lyin' like you're not aware
That I am here and you are there.

How about if I come **closer,**
You won't mind that, will you? **No, sir?**
I'll come near and you'll ignore—

ROAR! ROAR! ROAR!

ROAR! ROAR! ROAR!

Forget about my coming **closer,**
You're not lyin'—you said **"No, sir!"**

Lion, Lion, lurkin' there,
You're aware.
And you **care.**

M is for Monkey

What do you do with *a tail like that?*

You dangle at an **angle**,
You cling and also **fling**,
You reach across a **BREACH**,
You swing as if on **WING**.

And sometimes with *a tail like that*,
Although it's not a thrill,
Sometimes with a tail like that
You. Just. Sit. **STILL.**

N is for Newt

Newts **don't** wear **boots.**
But if they wore them,
And their boot-wearing feet
Were lopped,
If they tore them
Right off their legs,
Then what they would do
Is **GROW** those feet back.

They would. **It's TRUE.**

But those newly grown feet
Would **not** grow new **boots**
Because that is beyond
The **POWER** of Newts.

23

Octopus SQUEEZES
Where Octopus pleases,

Shape-shifting
Swim-drifting

Roaming every ocean,
Arms in constant **motion,**
Sucker-studded
Blue-blooded

Slime-oozing
Ink-diffusing
Tool-using
Coral-cruising

O

is for
Octopus

Octopus who pleases

Anyone who sees his

Boneless, brainy, squishy,
SQUEEZY self.

P is for Panda

Alone

Is Panda's way.

A life of **solitude.**

But not **the cubs!** Their way is to

CUDDLE.

Q

is for Quoll

Quite a **quiet** critter
Is the Eastern Quoll,
But then **darkness** falls
And:

Hiss!
Bark!
Cluck!
Chuck!

GROWL...

On a nighttime **prowl**
This **quiet** little critter

Has **quite a lot** to say.

Rhino takes a bath in dirt—
To be precise, in mud—
Splish, splash, splat, splurt,
Belly down, and **THUD!**

R
is for
Rhinoceros

Wriggle, roll, smear, smush,
Cool and lovely slop,
Rhino loves a water hole—
Belly down, and **PLOP!**

S

is for
Spider

BIG and hairy,

Venom-**scary,**

Itsy-bitsy,
Rainbow glitzy,

Toothy trapper,
Si**lky wrapper.**

Web site riders,
All are SPIDERS!

T

is for
Tapir

Hooves of rhino, **shape** of pig,
Elephant's **snout** (but not as big),

Baby ones wear zebra **coats.**
Grown-ups **climb** as well as goats.

Tapir is a creature made
As if a **zoo went on**

PARADE.

With horns so great and curly
And form so bulky-burly
The bulky-burly, great and curly
Urial

Grazes **hills** so
STEEP,

Pounces with a **LEAP—**

Is one **wild** ram of a
SHEEP.

U
is for
Urial

33

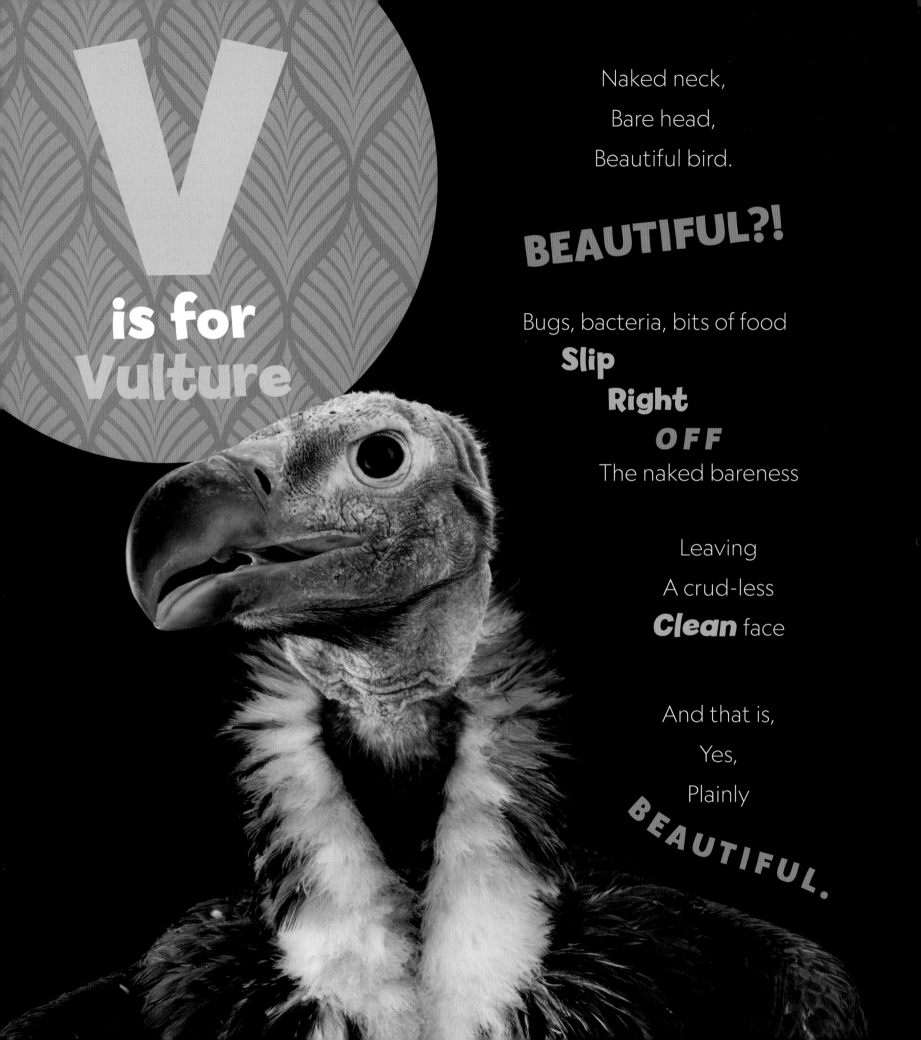

V is for Vulture

Naked neck,
Bare head,
Beautiful bird.

BEAUTIFUL?!

Bugs, bacteria, bits of food
Slip
Right
OFF
The naked bareness

Leaving
A crud-less
Clean face

And that is,
Yes,
Plainly
BEAUTIFUL.

What does Walrus
need?

Neither bed nor sled for this husky pinniped,
Not a toothbrush for those long, sharp tusks,

But ice, frozen **thick,**
Packed hard, like a **BRICK,**
Floating floes in the ocean,
Icy islands in motion—

Will the seas stay **cold?**
Will we help Walrus **hold**
On?

W

is for

Walrus

X is for Xenarthra

An Anteater, a Sloth, and an Armadillo walk into a **zoo . . .**

And the zookeeper says, **"Hello,** who are **you?"**

"We are Xenarthrans," the visitors say,

"From the planet Xenarthra. It's far, far away!"

But the zookeeper isn't so easily **fooled.**
In the matter of mammals, she's expertly schooled.

She knows these three animals live here on **Earth!**
They're part of a group, and they have been since birth,

A group called Xenarthra, which means that they've **got**
Some joints in their backs that others do **not.**

So . . .

If an Anteater, Sloth, or Armadillo tells you

That he's come here from space—now you'll know it's **not TRUE.**

There once was a Yabby

Down

Under

y

is for

Yabby

Who thought he could

vanquish

the

thunder

With claws he went **THWACK!**

At each **BOOM!** and each **cRACk!**

But could not tear thunder asunder.

Z is for Zebra and Zebra Finch

"I wish I had some

snazzy stripes,"

Finch twittered with a whimper.

"Sure, I've got these orange bits,

But mostly I feel gray."

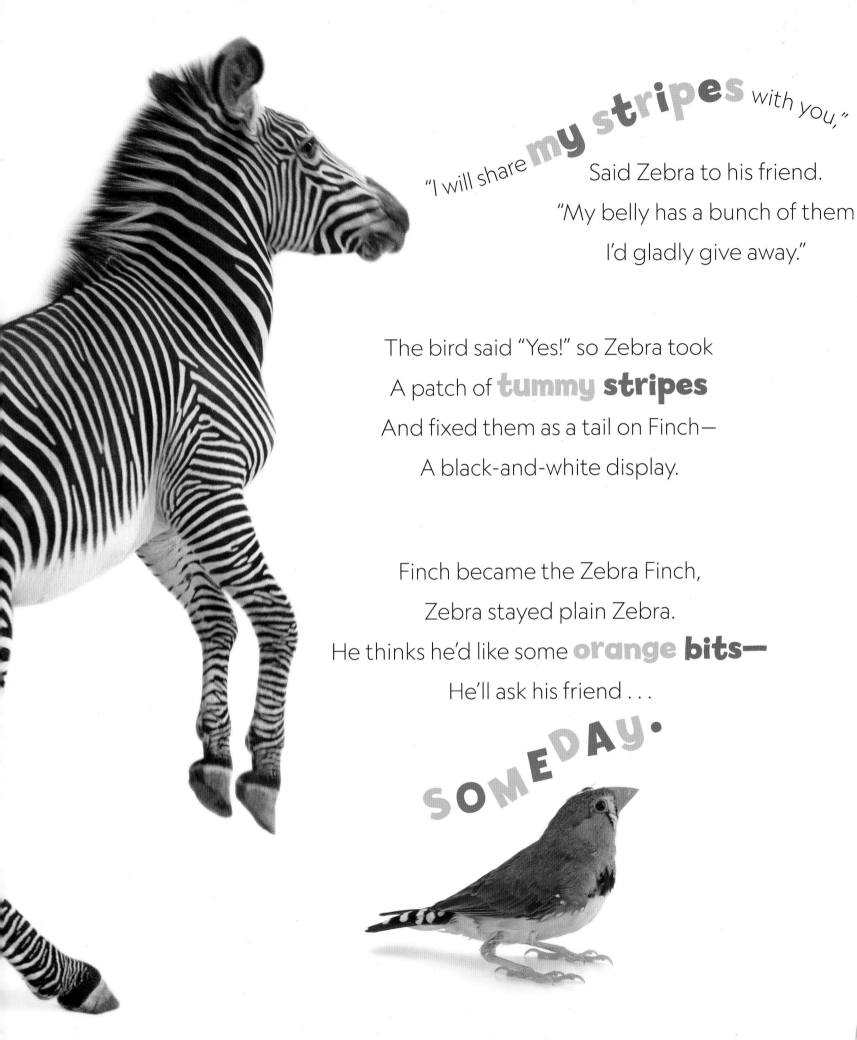

"I will share **my stripes** with you,"
Said Zebra to his friend.
"My belly has a bunch of them
I'd gladly give away."

The bird said "Yes!" so Zebra took
A patch of **tummy stripes**
And fixed them as a tail on Finch—
A black-and-white display.

Finch became the Zebra Finch,
Zebra stayed plain Zebra.
He thinks he'd like some **orange bits**—
He'll ask his friend . . .

SOMEDAY.

Spectacular creatures!

We can be
powerful or helpless,
thoughtful or heedless,
creative or destructive.
Will we be
protected or neglected?
The fate of living beings is
in human hands:
The air we breathe,
water, food, forests, grasslands
are shared.
Our habitats,
our actions—
So much depends on PEOPLE.

People!

So much depends on
our actions.
Our habitats
are shared:
water, food, forests, grasslands,
the air we breathe.
In human hands,
the fate of living beings is
protected or neglected.
Will we be
creative or destructive,
thoughtful or heedless,
powerful or helpless?
We can be SPECTACULAR CREATURES.

The **Animals** of the **Photo Ark ABC**

Dyeing poison frog
LC
Northern South America

Mallard duck
LC
North America, Europe, parts of Asia and Africa

Southern three-banded armadillo
NT
Parts of South America

Spotted jellyfish
NE
Coastal waters in Indian and Pacific Oceans

Oblong-winged katydid
NE
Parts of North America

Fiji crested iguana
CR
Fiji

Giant panda
VU
Central China

Cairns birdwing butterfly
LC
Parts of Australia

Red-tailed knobby newt
VU
China

Northern tamandua
(a type of anteater)
LC
Parts of North, South, and Central America

Southern three-banded armadillo
NT
Parts of South America

Grizzly bear
LC
Parts of North America

Mexican bluewing butterfly
NE
Parts of North and Central America

Large striped swordtail butterfly
LC
Parts of Africa

Pearl charaxes butterfly
NE
Africa

Eastern tiger swallowtail butterfly
NE
Parts of North America

Common green birdwing butterfly
LC
Parts of Asia, Australia, and Oceania

Plain tiger butterfly
NE
Parts of Asia, Australia, and Africa

Gray crowned crane (left)
EN
Parts of Africa

Black crowned cranes (center and right)
VU
Parts of Africa

Mallard duck
LC
North America, Europe, parts of Asia and Africa

Sumatran elephant
CR
Borneo and Sumatra

Southern orange-eyed tree frog
LC
Australia

Yellow-bellied poison frog
LC
Parts of Central and South America

Diablito frog
NT
Parts of South America

Fringed tree frog
LC
Parts of South America

Buckley's giant glass frog
VU
Parts of South America

Humpback grouper
DD
Coastal waters in the Pacific and Indian Oceans

Spotted hyenas
LC
Parts of Africa

Fiji crested iguana
CR
Fiji

Purple compass jellyfish
NE
Coastal waters in southeastern Atlantic Ocean

Oblong-winged katydids
NE
Parts of North America

Katanga lion
VU
Parts of Africa

Common woolly monkey
VU
Parts of South America

Red-tailed knobby newt
VU
China

Giant Pacific octopus
LC
Pacific Ocean

Giant pandas
VU
Central China

Eastern quoll
EN
Australia (Tasmania)

Sumatran rhinoceros
CR
Indonesia

Arboreal huntsman spider
NE
Equatorial Guinea

Cobalt blue tarantula
NE
Parts of Southeast Asia

Antilles pinktoe tarantula
NE
Martinique and Guadeloupe

Sutherland's funnel-web spider
NE
Australia

Pumpkin patch tarantula
NE
Parts of South America

Regal jumping spider
NE
Parts of North America

Malay tapir
EN
Parts of Southeast Asia

Transcaspian urial
VU
Parts of Asia

Lappet-faced vulture
EN
Parts of Africa and Asia

Pacific walrus
DD
Arctic regions of North America, Europe, and Asia

Brown-throated sloth
LC
Parts of Central and South America

Northern tamandua
(a type of anteater)
LC
Parts of North, South, and Central America

Six-banded armadillo
LC
Parts of South America

Common yabby
VU
Australian freshwater

Grevy's zebra
EN
Parts of Africa

Timor zebra finch
LC
Indonesia

Diademed sifaka
CR
Madagascar

Giant Pacific octopus
LC
Pacific Ocean

About IUCN Listings

The International Union for Conservation of Nature and Natural Resources (IUCN) is a global group dedicated to sustainability. The IUCN Red List of Threatened Species is a comprehensive collection of animal and plant species that have been analyzed according to their risk of extinction. Once evaluated, a species is placed into one of several categories. Each species' current IUCN status is listed beneath its name, along with where it can be found in the world.

EX: Extinct
EW: Extinct in the wild
CR: Critically endangered
EN: Endangered
VU: Vulnerable
NT: Near threatened
LC: Least concern
DD: Data deficient
NE: Not evaluated

A Note From the Photographer

When I was very young, my parents gave me a book full of amazing animal drawings. Many were of species I never knew existed. There was an aardvark, a monkey, and a tiger. Plus 23 more, one for each letter of the alphabet.

To say I was hooked on animals from that point on would be an understatement. I soon memorized the book, and I mean every square inch of it, with help from my parents, who read it to me every night. I truly believe it was that animal book of ABC's (along with one on dinosaurs, of course) that set me on the path I still follow today.

Following in that tradition is the *Photo Ark ABC*. Here you'll see a quoll, a tapir, and an urial sheep. Few people even know these animals exist, but in these pages and elsewhere, I hope to change that.

Largely a public education campaign, the Photo Ark is designed to get the world to care about all creatures, great and small. I started building it more than 15 years ago, sparked by the idea that most creatures are not famous like giraffes and lions. Instead, they're often small and hard to see, like minnows swimming in muddy water, soil-bound moles, or sparrows chirping from the treetops. And these days, many need our help.

By working with animals that are in human care, I'm able to bring many of the creatures otherwise hidden in nature into full view. I use studio lighting to bring out their true colors, and black and white backgrounds to eliminate all distractions and make intimate eye contact. Best of all, without any chance of size comparisons, the mouse is as big as the elephant, and every bit as important.

So far we have more than 11,000 animals photographed, with the goal of getting every single animal species in captivity. We have several thousand more to go, but it's worth it.

Without the Photo Ark, many animals I meet might never have their stories told, which is critical if we care about saving them and their habitats. The Photo Ark gives a voice to the voiceless, but beyond that, I believe that what happens to these animals will eventually happen to us. That's why it's vital we all be good stewards at every turn.

With *Photo Ark ABC*, my sincere hope is to inspire children not only to read, but to get hooked on animals, just as I was by the ABC book my parents read to me all those years ago. I want them to fall in love with the creatures in these pages and to care deeply about the natural world throughout their lives.

— **Joel Sartore**

The National Geographic Photo Ark is a multiyear effort with photographer Joel Sartore to photograph every captive species to inspire people to save those most vulnerable, while also funding conservation projects focused on those in most critical need of protection.

A Note From the Author

When I first encountered Joel Sartore's photographs, I felt as if I had discovered an album of pictures of . . . my family. I'm not suggesting that my family members are lucky enough to resemble the animals in the Photo Ark! Rather, the family feeling was about intimacy—a feeling of closeness. This sense of closeness deepened as my understanding of the threats many of these animals face deepened, threats frequently caused by actions taken by human beings. Two examples: Cutting down forests reduces the habitat for countless species. Our changing climate, worsened by our ceaseless burning of fossil fuels, has led to melting ice pack in the Arctic, depriving still more animals of their environment. Careless treatment of our shared planet is no way to treat family.

Even as I experienced the feeling that I was looking at a family album, I also felt a keen awareness of each animal's difference. The Spotted Hyena's Spotted Hyena-ness. The Common Yabby's Common Yabby-ness. The Lappet-Faced Vulture's—well, you get the idea. Every single creature in the Photo Ark is astounding. Fact: Grizzly bears may look slow and awkward because of their size, but they can outrun even the fastest human being. Fact: No zebra has the same stripe pattern as any other zebra. Fact: A hundred-pound octopus can squeeze through an opening the size of a quarter. Oh, I could go on and on!

The more I learned about the animals in this book (and those not in this book), the more my respect grew for their differences. We are all part of Earth's family, but we are not all the same, and this is awesome in the truest sense of that word: One feels awe, wonder, and admiration in contemplation of the biodiversity that surrounds us.

Which leads to my poetry choices in this book. I included a variety of forms to honor the animal world's variety. There is free verse (Crane, Grouper, Quoll, Urial, Vulture), a cinquain (Panda), a tanka (Hyena), and a pantoum (Frog). There are ballads (Armadillo, Bear/Butterfly, Xenarthra, Zebra/Zebra Finch). There is abstract poetry (Katydid) and a limerick (Yabby). The remaining animal poems are variations on rhyming forms.

The final poem is a reverso. In a reverso (invented by poet extraordinaire Marilyn Singer), the lines of the first half are repeated, in reverse, in the second half. The second half creates new meaning from the reversed lines. In my poem, the first half presents the animals' point of view; the second half is a human perspective. I wanted to signal my hope that people—especially young readers—will reverse at least some of the harm humans have inflicted on the animals with whom we share the planet. What wonderful new meaning that reversal would create.

— **Debbie Levy**

For my children, Cole, Ellen, and Spencer, who care deeply about the future of all species, great and small —JS

For my LLLs, distanced during the pandemic year, but never remote —DL

Published by National Geographic Partners, LLC.

Text Copyright © 2021 Debbie Levy
Photographs Copyright © 2021 Joel Sartore
Compilation Copyright © 2021 National Geographic Partners, LLC

Since 1888, the National Geographic Society has funded more than 14,000 research, conservation, education, and storytelling projects around the world. National Geographic Partners distributes a portion of the funds it receives from your purchase to National Geographic Society to support programs including the conservation of animals and their habitats. To learn more, visit natgeo.com/info.

For more information, visit nationalgeographic.com, call 1-877-873-6846, or write to the following address:

National Geographic Partners, LLC
1145 17th Street N.W.
Washington, DC 20036-4688 U.S.A.

For librarians and teachers: nationalgeographic.com/books/librarians-and-educators

More for kids from National Geographic: natgeokids.com

National Geographic Kids magazine inspires children to explore their world with fun yet educational articles on animals, science, nature, and more. Using fresh storytelling and amazing photography, *Nat Geo Kids* shows kids ages 6 to 14 the fascinating truth about the world—and why they should care. **kids.nationalgeographic.com/subscribe**

For rights or permissions inquiries, please contact National Geographic Books Subsidiary Rights: bookrights@natgeo.com

Designed by Sanjida Rashid
Author photograph by Lori Epstein

AUTHOR'S ACKNOWLEDGMENTS
Many thanks to Marfé Ferguson Delano, Sanjida Rashid, Lori Epstein, and the rest of the team at National Geographic Children's Books; to Michelle Harris, for her meticulous research; to Ben Hoffman, for fine-tuning; and to Joel Sartore, for letting me pair my words with his spectacular images.

PHOTOGRAPHER'S ACKNOWLEDGMENTS:
This work wouldn't happen without Dakota Altman, Sarah Booth, Alex Crisp, Daisha Marquardt, Emilia Roberts, Keri Smith, Krista Smith, Bryn Wells, and Rebecca Wright. And of course, there's my family, who for years have put up with life being, "All Photo Ark, All the Time!" My deepest thanks to all.

Hardcover ISBN: 978-1-4263-7246-9
Reinforced library binding ISBN: 978-1-4263-7247-6